THE ALLOTMENT GARDENER LOGBOOK

Gardening IS MY FAVORITE Therapy

Year :

JANUARY

THINGS TO DO

Task	Completed

PLANTS IN MY GARDEN

Plant Name	Number	Notes

Year :   **January**

WHAT I WILL HARVEST THIS MONTH

Produce	How Much	Consumed or Preserved

GARDEN NOTES

DRAWING BOARD

DRAWING BOARD

Year : January

Year : January

Year :

FEBRUARY

THINGS TO DO

Task	Completed

PLANTS IN MY GARDEN

Plant Name	Number	Notes

Year :   **February**

WHAT I WILL HARVEST THIS MONTH

Produce	How Much	Consumed or Preserved

GARDEN NOTES

DRAWING BOARD

DRAWING BOARD

February

Year :   **February**

Year :

MARCH

THINGS TO DO

Task	Completed

PLANTS IN MY GARDEN

Plant Name	Number	Notes

Year :   **March**

WHAT I WILL HARVEST THIS MONTH

Produce	How Much	Consumed or Preserved

GARDEN NOTES

Year :   **March**

DRAWING BOARD

Year :   **March**

DRAWING BOARD

Year :   **March**

Year :

APRIL

THINGS TO DO

Task	Completed

PLANTS IN MY GARDEN

Plant Name	Number	Notes

Year :   **April**

WHAT I WILL HARVEST THIS MONTH

Produce	How Much	Consumed or Preserved

GARDEN NOTES

DRAWING BOARD

DRAWING BOARD

Year :

MAY

THINGS TO DO

Task	Completed

PLANTS IN MY GARDEN

Plant Name	Number	Notes

Year :   **May**

WHAT I WILL HARVEST THIS MONTH

Produce	How Much	Consumed or Preserved

GARDEN NOTES

Year :   May

DRAWING BOARD

DRAWING BOARD

Year :   **May**

Year : **May**

Year :

JUNE

THINGS TO DO

Task	Completed

PLANTS IN MY GARDEN

Plant Name	Number	Notes

Year :   **June**

WHAT I WILL HARVEST THIS MONTH

Produce	How Much	Consumed or Preserved

GARDEN NOTES

Year :

June

DRAWING BOARD

DRAWING BOARD

Year :

JULY

THINGS TO DO

Task	Completed

PLANTS IN MY GARDEN

Plant Name	Number	Notes

Year :   **July**

WHAT I WILL HARVEST THIS MONTH

Produce	How Much	Consumed or Preserved

GARDEN NOTES

Year :   July

DRAWING BOARD

DRAWING BOARD

Year : July

Year : July

Year :

AUGUST

THINGS TO DO

Task	Completed

PLANTS IN MY GARDEN

Plant Name	Number	Notes

Year :   **August**

WHAT I WILL HARVEST THIS MONTH

Produce	How Much	Consumed or Preserved

GARDEN NOTES

DRAWING BOARD

DRAWING BOARD

Year :   **August**

Year :

SEPTEMBER

THINGS TO DO

Task	Completed

PLANTS IN MY GARDEN

Plant Name	Number	Notes

WHAT I WILL HARVEST THIS MONTH

Produce	How Much	Consumed or Preserved

GARDEN NOTES

Year :   **September**

DRAWING BOARD

DRAWING BOARD

Year : September

Year :   **September**

Year : **OCTOBER**

THINGS TO DO

Task	Completed

PLANTS IN MY GARDEN

Plant Name	Number	Notes

Year :   **October**

WHAT I WILL HARVEST THIS MONTH

Produce	How Much	Consumed or Preserved

GARDEN NOTES

DRAWING BOARD

DRAWING BOARD

Year :   **October**

Year :   **October**

Year :

NOVEMBER

THINGS TO DO

Task	Completed

PLANTS IN MY GARDEN

Plant Name	Number	Notes

Year :

WHAT I WILL HARVEST THIS MONTH

Produce	How Much	Consumed or Preserved

GARDEN NOTES

Year :   **November**

DRAWING BOARD

DRAWING BOARD

Year :   **November**

Year :　　　　　　　　　　　　　　　　　　　　　**November**

Year :

DECEMBER

THINGS TO DO

Task	Completed

PLANTS IN MY GARDEN

Plant Name	Number	Notes

Year :   **December**

WHAT I WILL HARVEST THIS MONTH

Produce	How Much	Consumed or Preserved

GARDEN NOTES

Year :

Year :   **December**

DRAWING BOARD

DRAWING BOARD

Year :   December

Year :   **December**

Year :   **December**

Printed in Great Britain
by Amazon

43015581R00064